Tsunamis

Written by Emily D

D1610496

Contents

Collins

What is a tsunami?

A tsunami is a fast, powerful, dangerous series of waves or wave.

Tsunamis are usually caused by a movement of the seabed which pushes the water above it into waves. The waves start small when they are out at sea; you wouldn't know it was a tsunami if you were in a boat floating on the water. But as the waves come towards the land, they increase in height and are powerful enough to bring large volumes of seawater inland causing flooding and devastation.

The word "tsunami" means "harbour waves" in Japanese. Tsunamis are more common in Japan so that's why we use their word for them.

tsunami waves hitting
the coast in Japan

3

Normal waves

Normal waves are caused by the wind pushing the water. The stronger the wind blows, the bigger the waves.

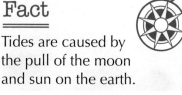

wind   wind   wind

tiny ripples   ripple   choppy sea   waves break

Waves are also created as **tides** slowly pull the ocean inland and away again every day.

Fact

Tides are caused by the pull of the moon and sun on the earth.

high tide

low tide

4

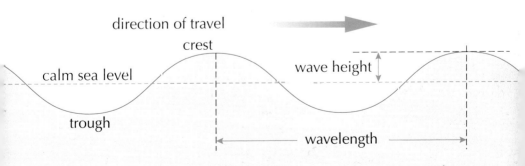
We can surf on normal waves.

We can measure waves in different ways. **Wavelength** is the distance between one wave and the next. Wave height is how high a wave is above calm sea level. Wave **period** is the time it takes between waves. The top of a wave is called the **crest** and lowest point between waves is called a **trough**.

direction of travel

crest

calm sea level

wave height

trough

wavelength

Tsunami waves

Tsunami waves are different to normal waves in several ways. Tsunamis are much faster out at sea; they can travel over 800 kilometres per hour. They also have a longer period – there can be two hours between each wave.

Typical tsunami wave versus normal wave		
	normal wave	tsunami wave
wave speed	eight to 100 kilometres per hour	800 to 965 kilometres per hour
wave period	three to 20 seconds apart	ten minutes to two hours apart
wavelength	30 to 200 metres apart	100 to 500 kilometres apart
wave height	one to seven metres	three to ten metres

A tsunami is usually between three and ten metres high when it reaches land, but occasionally it can be one giant wave 30 metres high called a bore.

Tsunamis are created in a different way to normal waves – they're created when a large volume of water is moved very quickly. It's a bit like throwing a pebble into a lake, and ripples travel away in all directions.

water ripples on a lake

Tsunami waves slow down as they move uphill towards the coast, and they also pile up and increase in height as the bottom of the wave slows down.

open ocean

sea floor

The shape of a bay, the slope of a beach and underwater features like **coral reefs** can change the impact of tsunami waves because they can change the speed and direction of waves as they move towards land.

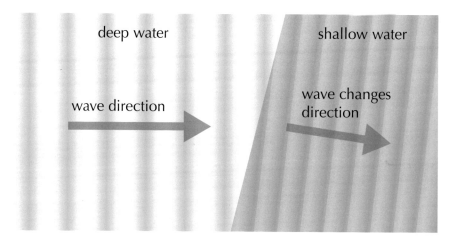

deep water

shallow water

wave direction

wave changes direction

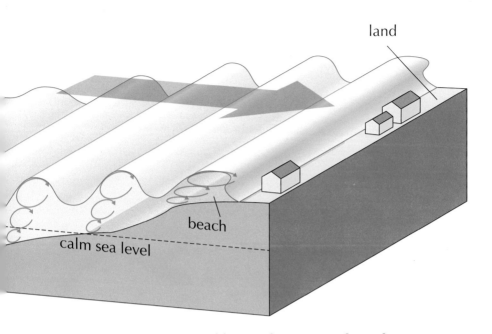

land

beach

calm sea level

Most tsunamis are caused by undersea **earthquakes**, but they can also be caused by **landslides**, **volcanoes** and even rocks from space, called meteorites, landing in the water.

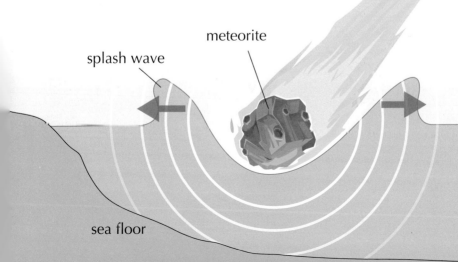

splash wave

meteorite

sea floor

Earthquakes and tsunamis

During an underwater earthquake, the seabed shakes and moves the water above it, making tsunami waves flow away from the area where the earthquake happens. We get earthquakes because the surface of planet Earth is made of giant pieces of slowly moving rock called plates. It's a bit like a jigsaw with all the pieces moving in different directions.

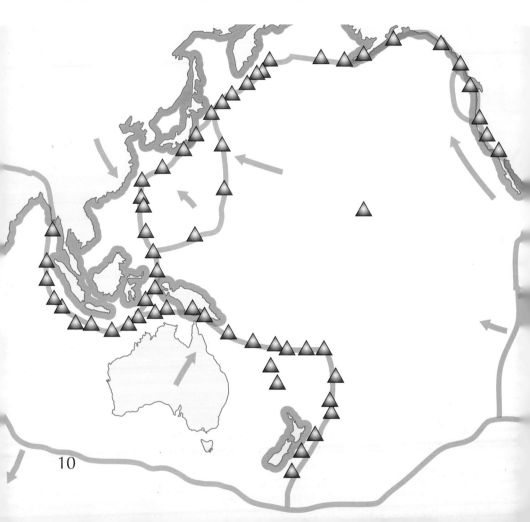

The plates sometimes get stuck together and stop moving for a while. When they finally move, this causes the ground to shake in a sudden violent movement of land known as an earthquake.

Most tsunamis take place around the Pacific Ocean where earthquakes and volcanoes are common.

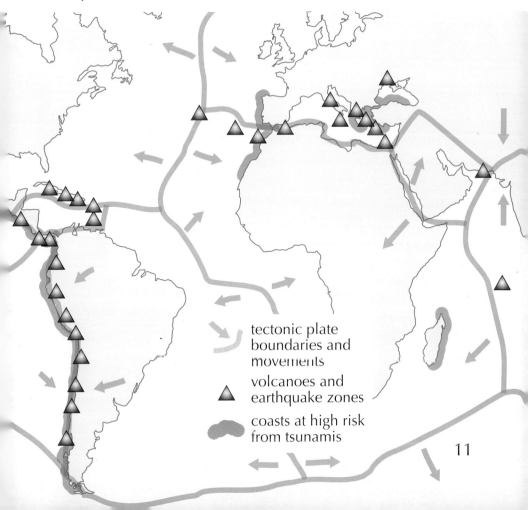

tectonic plate boundaries and movements

volcanoes and earthquake zones

coasts at high risk from tsunamis

Boxing Day Tsunami, 2004

On 26 December 2004, an earthquake off the coast of
Indonesia caused the most deadly tsunami in history.
One plate lifted up several metres, pushing large amounts
of water up and triggering tsunamis.

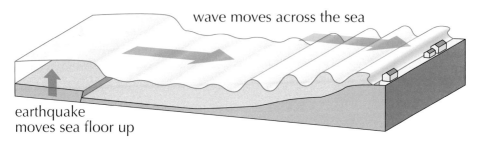

wave moves across the sea

earthquake
moves sea floor up

Tsunamis travelled in all directions across the Indian Ocean
hitting 14 countries with waves up to 30 metres high.

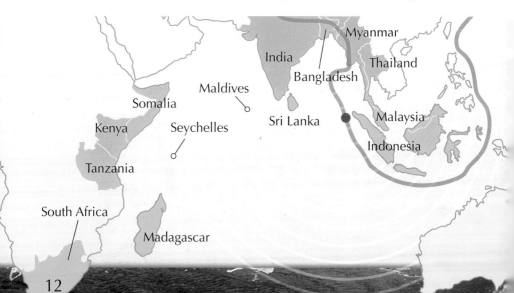

Fact

The earthquake lasted ten minutes and was the third biggest earthquake ever recorded.

Phuket, Thailand

Tsunami waves hit the island of Sumatra in Indonesia first because it was closest to the earthquake; waves reached Thailand 45 minutes later.

A quarter of a million people lost their lives. Crops were killed by saltwater, fishing boats were destroyed and two million people became homeless.

Fact

The tsunami waves were only one metre high out at sea.

Landslides and tsunamis

Tsunamis are occasionally caused when large quantities
of earth and rock slide down a slope into the sea in
a landslide. As rock and earth fall into the water, big waves
head away from the coast causing tsunamis when they
reach land.

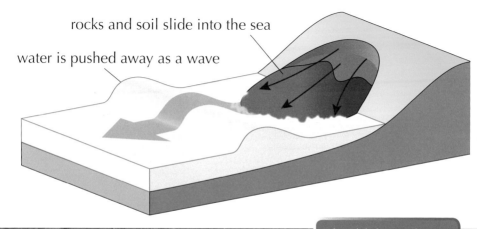

rocks and soil slide into the sea

water is pushed away as a wave

landslide in China

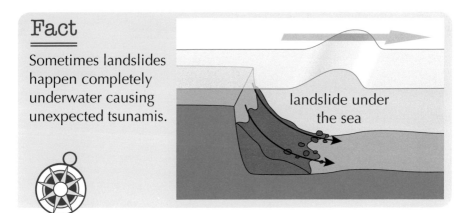

landslide under the sea

Landslides are often triggered by earthquakes that shake the land and make it unstable. They can also happen when volcanoes break up the land as they **erupt**.

Landslides sometimes happen when trees have been chopped down on a slope and there is heavy rain afterwards. Without tree roots and plants to hold the earth together, the earth can start to slide down the hill.

Another way landslides are created is in winter when water in cracks freezes and takes up more space. This pushes the rocks and earth apart and, if the water freezes and thaws a few times in a row, it could start a landslide.

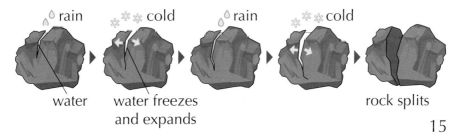

rain   cold   rain   cold

water   water freezes and expands   rock splits

Case study:

Lituya Bay, Alaska, 1958

In 1958, an earthquake triggered a rockfall in Lituya
Bay, Alaska. Rock and ice dropped into the bay from
a height of over 900 metres and made a huge splash
sending tsunami waves 500 metres high from the bay up
into the mountains above, in the world's highest tsunami.

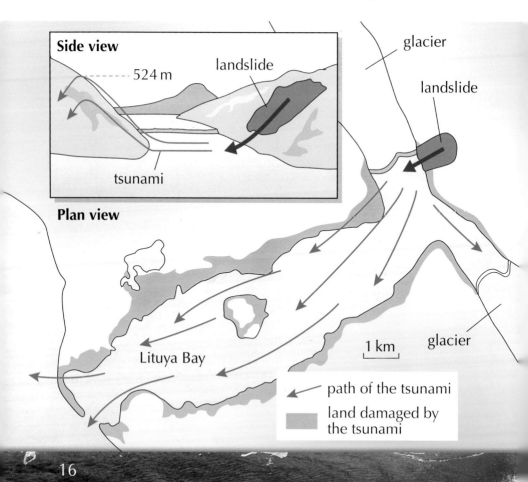

Side view

524 m

landslide

tsunami

glacier

landslide

Plan view

Lituya Bay

1 km

glacier

→ path of the tsunami

land damaged by
the tsunami

Lituya Bay, Alaska

This area is part of a **national park** and is surrounded by mountains. No one lives there, so there was very little loss of human life. The tsunami uprooted millions of trees and washed them away. Two fishermen in the bay were killed, and three others on Khantaak Island. Amazingly, four people in boats survived the tsunami.

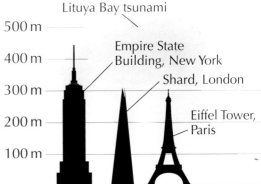

Lituya Bay tsunami

500 m
400 m — Empire State Building, New York
300 m — Shard, London
200 m — Eiffel Tower, Paris
100 m

Fact

Scientists discovered that a giant piece of rock 700 × 900 × 90 metres had crashed into Lituya bay.

Volcanoes and tsunamis

When hot liquid rock, gas and ash erupt from beneath the earth's surface in a volcano, it can trigger a tsunami in a number of ways.

When a volcano erupts, the rock surrounding the volcano can crack and shake and that can trigger a landslide or an **avalanche**. When land or snow falls quickly into nearby water, it can cause a tsunami.

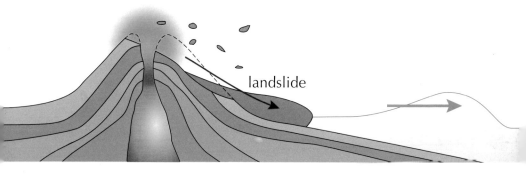

landslide

Eruptions of underwater volcanoes can push the water up quickly creating tsunamis.

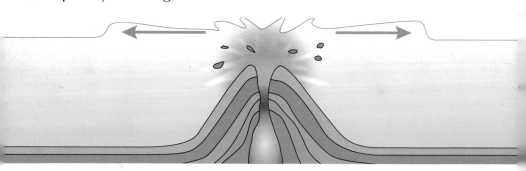

If a volcanic island erupts and explodes into the sea, the explosion can send tsunami waves in all directions, including to nearby islands.

Cape Verde Island collapsed around 73,000 years ago causing a mega tsunami.

Krakatoa, 1883

In 1883, two-thirds of the island of Krakatoa in Indonesia collapsed into the sea during a volcanic eruption. Hot gas, mud and ash hit the water at great speed as the island exploded. The series of explosions sent ash 27 kilometres up into the air and triggered tsunamis in the water.

The nearby town of Merak and many other coastal towns and villages were destroyed by waves 46 metres high. Over 35,000 people were killed.

the remains of Krakatoa Island today

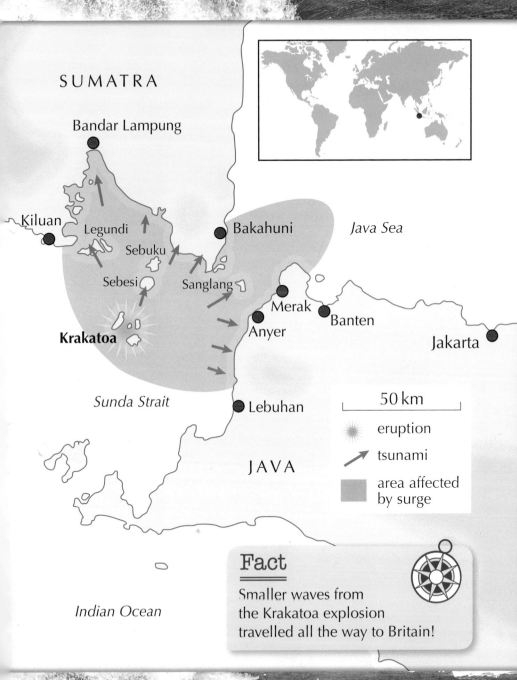

SUMATRA

Bandar Lampung

Kiluan

Legundi

Sebuku

Sebesi

Sanglang

Krakatoa

Bakahuni

Java Sea

Merak

Banten

Anyer

Jakarta

Sunda Strait

Lebuhan

JAVA

50 km

☀ eruption

↗ tsunami

area affected by surge

Indian Ocean

Fact

Smaller waves from the Krakatoa explosion travelled all the way to Britain!

Predicting tsunamis

Three-quarters of all tsunamis start in the Pacific Ocean. Hawaii lies in the middle of the Pacific Ocean and is surrounded on all sides by plate boundaries where earthquakes occur.

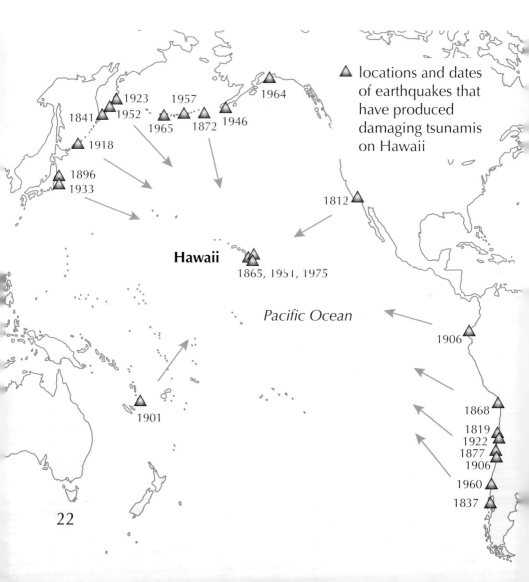

△ locations and dates of earthquakes that have produced damaging tsunamis on Hawaii

1923
1957
1964
1841
1952
1965   1872 1946
1918
1896
1933
1812
Hawaii
1865, 1951, 1975
Pacific Ocean
1906
1901
1868
1819
1922
1877
1906
1960
1837

Because of the danger of tsunamis, Hawaii and the surrounding countries now have a **monitoring** system in place to help predict tsunamis and warn people to get to higher ground.

Firstly, earthquakes are monitored all around the world. If an earthquake is recorded, scientists know a tsunami might follow.

Secondly, **buoys** floating in the water and **sensors** on the seabed continually measure the weight and height of water passing. If it changes because of a tsunami, signals are sent to the land and warning sirens go off to evacuate the area in danger.

communications satellite

radio signals

control centre

surface buoy

Not drawn to scale

bottom pressure sensor

Fact

The batteries in an ocean tsunami detector last four years!

acoustic signals

anchor weights

seabed

Living with tsunamis

Mangroves are forests that grow in saltwater on the coast around the Pacific Ocean. They provide an amazing natural defence against waves, reducing their height and strength before they reach land. Unfortunately, we have chopped down most of the mangrove forests on planet Earth, but scientists are now trying to replant the forests to help save lives in the event of a tsunami.

replanting mangroves

mangrove forest

This 14-metre sea wall in Fudai, Japan protected the whole village from a tsunami.

As well as natural defences, man-made defences have been successful in saving people from tsunamis. Large concrete sea walls are being built to shield towns from the waves.

Many parts of the world now have tsunami warning systems and **evacuation** plans in place so everyone knows what to do in an emergency. For example, people know to move to higher ground if they see the ocean go back an unusually long way because it's a sign a tsunami could follow.

Living after tsunamis

Immediately after a devastating tsunami, people all over the world watch news reports and are moved to give money to help with the rescue and rebuilding of the places affected.

Volunteers fly in to help distribute medicine and food. They also help people to find shelter and get connected to electricity and clean water.

Charities advise people and give them money to start new businesses because everything people own can be destroyed by a tsunami.

Banda Aceh on Sumatra island, before …

Communities work together to help each other to start over again. Even now, many years after the 2004 Boxing Day Tsunami in Indonesia, homes and communities are still being rebuilt. But now, tsunami monitoring systems are in place all over the world to help warn people of the approach of a tsunami in the future, hopefully giving them a greater chance of survival.

Waiting for a meal in a tsunami relief camp.

… after

Glossary

avalanche   a sudden rush of rocks, snow or ice down a mountain

buoys   round, bright, colourful floats used in the water

coral reefs   important underwater areas of sea animals that stay in one place and look like colourful plants

crest   the tip of a wave

earthquakes   the shaking of the earth

erupt   to burst out

evacuation   the removal of people from a dangerous place

landslides   when land falls down a slope

monitoring   keeping watch or keeping track of something over time

national park   an area of protected natural beauty containing important plants and animals

period   the time it takes between waves

sensors   instruments that measure something

tides   the rise and fall of the sea, twice a day, due to the attraction of the moon and the sun

trough   the lowest point between waves

volcanoes   the places where lava, gas and ash erupt

wavelength   the distance between two wave crests

Index

Tsunamis – causes and protection

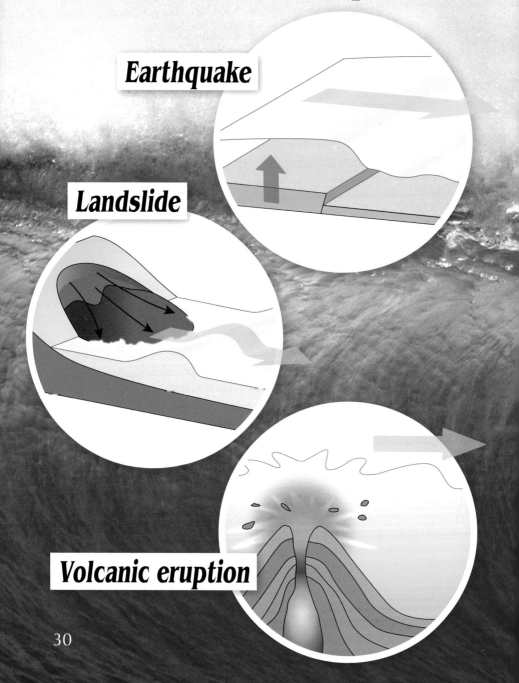

Earthquake

Landslide

Volcanic eruption

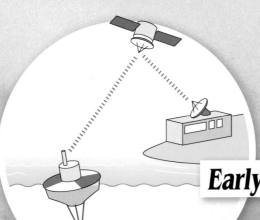

Early warning

Man-made defences

Natural defences

Ideas for reading

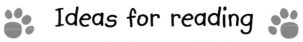

Written by Clare Dowdall, PhD
Lecturer and Primary Literacy Consultant

Reading objectives:
- retrieve and record information from non-fiction
- read books that are structured in different ways
- discuss their understanding and explain the meaning of words in context

Spoken language objectives:
- give well-structured descriptions, explanations and narratives for different purposes

Curriculum links: Geography – Human geography

Resources: ICT for research, materials for designing and making a poster

Build a context for reading
- Introduce the word *tsunami* and ask children to suggest what it means.
- Introduce the book by looking at the cover photograph and reading from the blurb.
- Challenge children to make predictions by answering the questions raised.

Understand and apply reading strategies
- Look at the word *tsunami*. Ask children what is challenging about reading and spelling this word.
- Read through the contents with the children, helping them to notice how the book is organised.
- Discuss which chapters might provide the answers to the questions raised in the blurb.